Contents

Be safe

You should be able to have a go at everything in your *Brownie Annual*, but sometimes it is a good idea to get some help. When you see this symbol, ask an adult if they can lend a hand.

Be safe

Web safe

This symbol means you should follow your Brownie Web Safe Code. To remember it, look at page 51 in your *Brownie Annual*.

Web safe

Badges!

Look out for this sign. If you enjoyed the activity on that page, you might like to try the badge too!

Badge link

Time capsule

Look out for time capsules throughout your *Brownie Annual* – they contain cool titbits about Brownies and general history from the last 100 years.

Look out for me!

WE DISCOVER, WE GROW
Girlguiding

Published by Girlguiding
17–19 Buckingham Palace Road
London SW1W 0PT
info@girlguiding.org.uk
www.girlguiding.org.uk

© The Guide Association 2013

Girlguiding is an operating name of The Guide Association. Registered charity number 306016. Incorporated by Royal Charter.

ISBN 978-0-85260-253-9
Girlguiding order code: 6005

Printed by Butler Tanner & Dennis Ltd

Editor: Mariano Kälfors
Writers: Laura Burke, Helen Davis, Jessica Feehan, Rosie Fletcher, Mariano Kälfors, Daniel Mckeown, Helen Mortimer, Amy Price, Alison Shaw, Ruth Stone, Helen Thomas
Cover Designer: Helen Davis
Designers: Angie Daniel, Helen Davis, Yuan Zhuang
Production Controller: Wendy Reynolds
Photographer: Abi Howson
Brownie Programme Adviser: Helen Channa

Illustrations courtesy of Shutterstock unless otherwise stated. Photography © The Guide Association unless otherwise stated.

Girlguiding would like to thank the 2nd Chigwell Brownies for their help with this Annual.

Users are reminded that during the lifespan of this publication there may be changes to:
• Girlguiding's policy
• legal requirements
• British Standards
which will affect the accuracy of the information contained within these pages.

MIX
Paper from responsible sources
FSC® C023561

My Big Brownie Birthday

Planning to celebrate the Big Brownie Birthday? You're not alone! Here are some of the great things Brownies will be getting up to. Maybe you're doing some of them too!

Challenge

Like all Brownie adventures, the Big Brownie Birthday has a challenge for Brownies. By now, you and your unit will have heard about the Big Brownie Birthday Challenge. Maybe you've even started planning how to complete it and get the badge!

Star Quest

The Big Brownie Birthday Star Quest is an adventure in a day! Someone has stolen all the stars above the Southern Hemisphere, and it's up to Brownies to get them back! If you're among the many Brownies getting together for a Star Quest cosmic adventure, expect time travel, fun activities, challenges and stars! Lots of stars!

Stay Away

What's better than a party? A party with a sleepover of course! Big Brownie Birthday Stay Aways will be happening everywhere. In meeting halls, on camps, at zoos, museums and theme parks – wherever Brownies can think of that would be great for a Stay Away!

World Centres

Heard of Sangam (India), Our Chalet (Switzerland) or Our Cabaña (Mexico)? They are three guiding treasures – World Centres where guiding girls from around the world can stay and make global friends. But Brownies won't need to travel so far, because the World Centres are coming to the UK for the Big Brownie Birthday! Without leaving these shores, Brownies will experience international travel, and the food, customs and languages of other cultures.

adventures

Euro Hop

The Big Brownie Birthday Euro Hop is a Brownie adventure with a European flavour. Intrepid Brownies will be packing their passports, berets and other continental essentials for a fabulous holiday across the Channel to France and Belgium. Ooh la la!

You are invited to...

Event:
Celebrate

Day:
22 February 2014

Where:
Everywhere

Occasion:
To join Brownies and other guiding friends to celebrate World Thinking Day 2014

RSVP

Party!

Any excuse to have a party is always great! And the Big Brownie Birthday is a really good excuse to celebrate! Brownie units everywhere will be having parties big and small – maybe your unit will too!

Have you and your friends come up with your own special way to celebrate the Big Brownie Birthday? Write down what you're doing!

We are:

What's in a name?

Nicknames, secret names, funny names! How many do you have?

Your names

Hi! My nam is ...

What your friends call you:

Alex

What your family calls you:

muggling
Poppet
munchcin

Your first name, spelled backwards:

xelA

XIS

SEINWORB

LERRIUQS

If you had super powers, what would your superhero name be?

Avlex

How many points is your name worth?

In the board game Scrabble, each letter is worth a different number of points. Add up the score from each letter of your name to find your total. For example Joy (J + O + Y) is 8 + 1 + 4 = 13. What's your score? Your friends? Your family? Your pet!

Letter	1	1	8	=	1	4	2	1	1	=	1	1	8	2	1	2	3	1	1	Total
Score	4	1	4	4	7	3	1	8	4	2	2	1	3	1	1	1	1	7		

A: 1	F: 4	K: 5	P: 3	U: 1	Z: 10
B: 3	G: 2	L: 1	Q: 10	V: 4	
C: 3	H: 4	M: 3	R: 1	W: 4	
D: 2	I: 1	N: 1	S: 1	X: 8	
E: 1	J: 8	O: 1	T: 1	Y: 4	

Example 1: Jazzy (J+A+Z+Z+Y)
8+1+10+10+4=33

Example 2: Xaqira (X+A+Q+I+R+A)
8+1+10+1+1+1=22

22+8+9+17
+12+4+1

8

Does your name say anything about you?

Write out your name in full, including any middle names. How many words can you make using only these letters? Write them here.

1914 Brownie section created. Early names and suggested names for the section before it became Brownies include Rosebuds, Junior Tenderfoots, Buds, Bees, Heather Bells, Kittens, Diddies, Juniors, Mice and Rats!

Do any of them describe you?

What do you stand for?

An acronym is a word in which each letter stands for another word. So if you go diving, you might need Self-Contained Underwater Breathing Apparatus – or 'Scuba' gear!

Can you make your name into an acronym by finding words that begin with each letter? 'Helen' might become 'Happy Elephants Limbo Every Night'. What about the other girls in your Six? Write down your favourites below.

Lend a hand

Have some fun with the Brownie special saying!

1915 'Lend a hand' is adopted by the Brownie section as its special saying.

Good Turns

Can you come up with some Good Turns for every letter in the Brownie special saying? We've put in some ideas to help you get started!

Look after your brother or sister, or help look after a pet.
Explain something to someone at school who's new or looks lost.
N
Don't leave things messy – tidy up as you go!
A
Help cheer up someone who's not feeling well by making something for them or writing them a letter.
A
N
D

Can your hands talk?

Even if you don't know sign language, you'll know all these ways to speak with your hands.

Clapping/thumbs up – say 'well done' to someone who has tried really hard.
Hold hands – be a good friend to someone who is upset.
Wave – make someone feel welcome by saying hello!
Put your hand up – ask lots of questions.
Finger on lips – be a good listener.

Can you think of any more ways your hands could help someone? Draw them below.

Illustrated by Nancy Meyers

How handy!

Make a handbook with a difference to record all your Good Turns!

Badge link

Communicator

What to do

1 Fold the paper in half, and in half again.

You will need

- sheet of A4 coloured paper
- pen or pencil
- scissors
- stapler

2 Place your hand on the folded paper and draw around it.

3 Cut carefully around the outline through all four layers of paper. You should now have four identical hand shapes.

Be safe

4 Staple through the wrist part of your paper hands, so that each hand becomes a page.

5 Every time you do a Good Turn (or someone does one for you), write it on one of the fingers. Soon your book will be full of great Good Turn ideas that you can share with your Six!

Badge quiz

How well do you know your
Brownie badges?

1

Which Brownie badge asks you to make
a scrapbook of the kind of thing you think
Brownies will be doing in ten years' time?

a) Brownie traditions ✔
b) Brownie skills
c) Artist

2

If you designed a model building that
could survive an earthquake and
tasted lemonade, water,
yoghurt and toothpaste,
which badge would you
be working towards?

a) Designer ✔
b) Five senses
c) Science investigator

3

Which badge is this?

a) Tap dancer
b) Shoe collector
c) Sports ✔

4

Which Brownie badge has pictures
of a camera, needle and thread,
and a rollerskate on it?

a) Extreme sports
b) Hobbies ✔
c) Filmmaker

5

How many
badges are there
that begin with
the letter 'F'?
What are they?

6 If you like acting and drama, which of these badges might you choose? Crime prevention, Entertainer or Discovering faith?

7 Which is the only Brownie badge with a 'Z' in its name?

Stargazer

8 What badge would you like to try next?

grand + o animals

Check page 76 to see how you did!

1917 Badges for Brownies to earn are introduced.

To help you answer these questions, look at the *Brownie Badge Book* or go to the Brownie website at www.girlguiding.org.uk/brownies – it's full of games, stories and competitions too!

Web safe

13

Glasgow games

There will be an exciting festival of sport this summer – the Glasgow 2014 Commonwealth Games!

What's on?

The Commonwealth Games is held every four years, like the Olympics, and takes entrants from countries in the Commonwealth. The athletes will compete at athletics, cycling, boxing and many other sports. There are also some sports that are not in the Olympics, like rugby sevens and lawn bowls.

1930 The first Commonwealth Games is held in Ontario, Canada.

Who's coming?

There will be teams from some huge countries, including India, Canada, South Africa and Australia. There will also be teams from places like Niue, Vanuatu and Norfolk Island, small islands in the South Pacific. Unlike at the Olympics, there will be no Team GB – instead, there will be separate teams from England, Scotland, Wales and Northern Ireland. There will also be teams from Guernsey, Jersey and the Isle of Man.

The official tartan of Glasgow 2014, with designer Aamir Mehmood.

Clyde by Guide!

The mascot for Glasgow 2014 is Clyde the Thistle, named after the River Clyde, which flows through Glasgow. Clyde was designed by Beth Gilmour, a Guide from Lanarkshire!

Profile: Triathlon

Triathlon is a very demanding sport in which athletes must swim, cycle and run to complete the course. There will be an exciting new triathlon event at Glasgow 2014 – the Mixed Relay. Teams will have two men and two women, who will each complete a short triathlon course before passing on to a teammate.

Badge link

Sports

Cyclist

World cultures

DB Case Files: The Lost Mascots

Help Detective Brownie match the mascots to the correct Commonwealth Games.

1. 1978 Edmonton
2. 1982 Brisbane
3. 1986 Edinburgh
4. 1990 Auckland
5. 1994 Victoria

6. 1998 Kuala Lumpur
7. 2002 Manchester
8. 2006 Melbourne
9. 2010 Delhi

Answers on page 76!

The next Commonwealth Games will be on the Gold Coast in Australia in 2018.

a) b) c) d) e)

f) g) h) i)

A brief history of flight

Between 200,000 and 300,000 planes take off every day from over 40,000 airports around the world, but it wasn't always that way!

Epic fail

In Greek mythology (so it's not a true story) a boy called Icarus is able to fly thanks to wings made by his father from bird feathers. Unfortunately, Icarus flies a little too close to the sun and the glue holding the feathers together melts in the heat. You can guess the rest.

A load of hot air

The Montgolfier brothers from France noticed that hot air rises in the atmosphere. They came up with the great idea of building a giant hot air balloon to carry people. The first hot air balloon journey with passengers took place on 21 November 1783. With the help of wind, the balloon flew for 5 miles in 25 minutes. Bravo!

Doing it the Wright way

The Wright brothers, Wilbur and Orville, were the first people to successfully fly an airplane. They did it on 17 December 1903 in Kitty Hawk, North Carolina, USA, with a plane they built themselves. They managed four flights that day. The first, by Orville, lasted 12 seconds and managed a distance of 37 metres. The last flight, by Wilbur, lasted 59 seconds and reached 259 metres!

Channel challenge

Less than six years after the Wright brothers made flying history, Frenchman Louis Blériot went one better and flew his plane across the English Channel! Using wooden propellers and bicycle wheels! The historic flight from Calais to Dover took place on 25 July 1909 and lasted 36 minutes and 30 seconds. Allez!

© Getty Images

LA TRAVERSÉE DU PAS-DE-CALAIS EN AÉROPLANE
Blériot atterrit sur la falaise de Douvres

All aboard!

It wasn't long before everyone was taking to the skies! The first passenger flight service, between London and Paris, was launched on 25 August 1919. It flew from Hounslow Heath, near today's London Heathrow Airport, and was operated by what later became British Airways.

Atlantic Amelia

In 1932 American Amelia Earhart became the first woman to fly alone across the Atlantic Ocean. She repeated the extraordinary flight first made by Charles Lindbergh in 1927. Amelia set off from Newfoundland, Canada, on 20 May and landed 14 hours and 56 minutes later near Derry, Northern Ireland. Outstanding!

The sky's the limit

The largest passenger plane in the world is (currently) the Airbus A380. It can whisk up to 853 passengers 8,000 miles away in just 16 hours – that's nearly from the UK to Australia!

© Alamy

Lucky se7en

Life (and Brownies!) begins at seven! Find out what some young women in guiding were like at that age!

When I was 7, I wanted to be a giraffe because I was so short!
Roxy, Leader, Downs Senior Section

When I was 7, I loved ballet because I could let out my energy and make lots of new friends.
Jess, Young Leader, 3rd Margate St John's Guides

When I was 7, I wanted to be a postwoman, a lifeguard and a waitress – all at the same time!
Amanda, Crofton District Rangers

When I was 7, I wanted to be a vet because of a trip to a farm with my Brownie unit.
Kathryn, Young Leader, 1st Lower Kingswood Rainbows & Guides

When I was 7, I wanted to be a police officer. I went around with foil handcuffs and 'arrested' everyone!
Emily, 1st Partridge Green Brownies

Did you know?

There are seven musical notes – 'do', 're', 'mi', 'fa', 'so', 'la', 'ti'.

1937 Age girls can join Brownies is lowered from eight to seven.

Did you know?

Some people, such as Germans, believe that cats have seven lives, not nine!

Did you know?

A common ladybird has seven spots.

Did you know?

The human eye can see seven stellar (starry) objects in our solar system – the sun, the moon, Mars, Mercury, Jupiter, Venus and Saturn.

Did you know?

The 2012 Girls' Attitudes Survey found that 7- to 11-year-olds were happiest out of everyone, with a total of 94 per cent feeling happy or quite happy.

Space to grow

It was 1940 and the Second World War was well under way. One evening at Brownies, their Leader, Dot, had some very, very worrying news to share. 'Since war has been declared, food shortages have been worsening. There just isn't enough food to go around and we must all do our bit to help out.'

'But what can I possibly do to help?' squeaked one tearful-looking Brownie, Maggy. 'I am only one small Brownie and this news is huuuuge!'

'On our own we might feel very small, but when we get together with our Brownie friends we can make a difference.' said Dot.

'I'm sure we can come up with an idea if we all put our thinking caps on, I'm sure we can!' piped up Amy.

'Brownies together!' cried out Neesha.

'My mum says that more heads are better than one!' added Kate.

'I'm hungry…' moaned Tilly.

'Let's grow some vegetables!' exclaimed a group of Brownies.

'Oh, yes, let's!' agreed everyone else… except for Lucy, who didn't look very happy.

'Excellent!' replied Dot. 'Let's get started!'

'We need a space to grow our vegetables, where will we ever find one?' asked Betty, looking disheartened.

'That's easy,' said Dot, 'look at all the space we have at our unit meeting place – we'll turn it into a vegetable patch. Lots of public patches of ground are being turned into vegetable plots to help – even parks.'

A few weeks and packets of seeds later…

'This is messy!' said Neesha.

'This is fun!' said Lou.

'Good, messy fun!' said Dot. 'Not too much water, Amy! We don't want the carrots to drown!'

Lucy sat quietly on the garden wall. 'I don't even like vegetables,' she muttered. 'I don't want to help.'

'Come on Lucy,' coaxed Dot, 'give it a try and see how you get on. If you haven't done it before, how do you know you won't like it?'

'Oh, all right,' Lucy said slowly. 'Just so long as I don't have to eat them!'

'We all need fresh vegetables to eat to help us stay happy and healthy, whether we're playing or learning, war or no war,' said Dot.

'I prefer cake,' sulked Lucy.

'Well, there's definitely not much of that around at the moment,' replied Dot, 'but I can show you how to make vegetables into a delicious cake, would you like that?'

1939-45 Brownies contribute enthusiastically to the war effort, including raising money from cleaning shoes, growing vegetables, donating pocket money, giving away toys and collecting clothes.

'Veg in a cake?' snorted Lucy. 'Impossible!'

'You'll love it! I promise!' grinned Dot (and no one in Brownies ever makes a Promise lightly).

Before long Lucy was laughing and getting stuck in with the rest of them, and thoroughly enjoying the veggie patch project.

A few months and lots of Brownie hard work later....

'Wow! Look at our vegetables!' cried Lou. 'They're huge!'

'You've all worked very hard, you should be very proud of yourselves,' smiled Dot.

'It's been so much fun, it hasn't felt like work at all!' said Amy.

'True,' agreed Neesha, 'and it's really helped take my mind off the war – that used to really scare me, but I've had this to think about lately.'

'Don't the tomatoes look delicious?' declared Kate.

'Yuck!' said Lucy. 'Thank goodness we're giving them all away, though I don't know who will ever want to eat them! I thought not having enough veg was a good thing! And you've all gone and planted loads!'

The Brownies set to work harvesting their vegetables and couldn't believe how many there were! They all felt so proud as they wheeled them around the neighbourhood in the wheelbarrows and prams they had borrowed.

'Get your veg! Grown by Brownies for you! Lots of carrots!' they all cried out.

People poured out of their houses to see the spectacle and collect their vegetables. 'Thank you so much!' they all exclaimed. 'What a difference this will make! What would we have done without you?'

'They came up with the idea all by themselves,' said Dot.

'Well done to the Brownies!' cried the crowd that had gathered on the village green.

'Girls can do anything – right, Brownies?' called out Dot.

'YES!' the Brownies all replied together, before heading home to wash the mud off their smiling faces.

As for Lucy, she didn't utter a word... she was too busy munching on her BEETROOT CAKE!

Love food, hate waste!

True chefs know that leftovers are just the start of a great meal!

Mediterranean tartlets (serves 6)

Turn leftover roasted vegetables from last night's dinner into tonight's tasty supper!

You will need

* 1 sheet (375g) ready-rolled puff pastry
* a little flour
* 190g jar of red or green pesto
* about 170g leftover roasted vegetables (such as peppers, onions, courgettes, artichokes)
* 12 slices of chorizo or 6 slices of Parma ham (optional)
* 200g of your favourite cheese (try mozzarella, feta or brie)
* a little olive oil (for drizzling)
* salt and pepper
* a little milk (to glaze)

* baking tray lined with greaseproof paper
* sharp knife
* tablespoon
* pastry brush

What to do

Be safe

1 Preheat the oven to 200°C/gas mark 6. Lay out the ready-rolled puff pastry on a lightly floured surface and use the knife to divide it into six squares. Lay each square on the lined baking tray.

1940 Food rationing in the UK begins, and people become creative with food, including carrots on sticks to replace lollies!

22

2 Spread a tablespoon of pesto on to the centre of each pastry square, leaving a 1cm edge all the way around.

3 Top each pastry square with a couple of tablespoons of the leftover roasted vegetables and the sliced meat (if using), and top with cheese.

4 Drizzle the topping with a little olive oil and season with salt and pepper. Brush a little milk around the edge of each pastry square.

Top tips!

* If you cut more squares from your pastry (12 instead of 6) you can make mini Mediterranean tartlets – great party food!
* The tartlets are also delicious served cold – perfect to take on a picnic.

5 Bake in the oven for 20 to 25 minutes or until the pastry puffs up and is golden brown and the cheese has melted.

Recycling is fun!

Egg carton flowers

These flowers will never need to be watered and are a fun way to recycle cardboard egg cartons while cheering up a table.

You will need

* ✳ empty 12-egg carton
* ✳ poster paints
* ✳ paintbrushes
* ✳ newspaper
* ✳ 12 green pipe cleaners
* ✳ scissors
* ✳ vase (to put your flowers in)

What to do

1 Carefully tear each cup (the part that holds the egg) out of the carton, so you have 12 cups.

Even after the war, food and supplies are still scarce in the 1940s and people recycle everything, including making underwear out of old parachutes!

2 Using the poster paints, paint each cup inside and out in bright colours. You could even paint each cup a different colour on the inside to the outside. Leave your painted cups to dry on a sheet of newspaper.

3 When your painted cups are dry, use a pipe cleaner to poke a small hole through the bottom of each one. Insert a pipe cleaner through the hole in each cup and twist it slightly at the top to keep it in place. The pipe cleaner will be the flower stem.

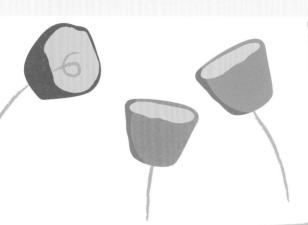

Top tips!

Decorate the centre of each flower by gluing on beads or sequins.

4 With a pair of scissors, make six or seven cuts from the edge of your cup towards the centre and fan out each section to make the petals for your flower.

Be safe

5 Each cup has now turned into a beautiful flower! Arrange your stems in the vase and display them where everyone can enjoy them.

Putting on a display

Fancy yourself as an exhibition designer? Here are some useful tips to help you get started.

Visit the idea bank

Sit down with your friends and spend 15 to 20 minutes scribbling down whatever comes into your heads. Look through any old newspapers and magazines you have as well for more inspiration. You could also tear off bits you like to glue with your notes, but make sure you have adult permission to do so.

Get the facts

What is your display for? What kind of display will it be? What materials can you use to create it? Who is helping you make it? Start your project by getting all your important information together first. When you have this, then you can roll up your sleeves and get to work.

Draw it

Work out your design on paper first. Make as many rough sketches as you need until you're happy with it. Show it to friends, Leaders and family too for comments and suggestions.

Let's celebrate **The Big Brownie Birthday**

Posters

Making a poster? Think about fun shapes for it – it doesn't have to be a plain rectangle! You could use craft materials too. Using pictures? Have just one or two really good, large, eye-catching ones, rather than lots of little ones. Make the writing quite big too so it's easy to read, even from a distance.

Windows

Creating a window display? Maybe for your favourite charity shop? Do some research and look around to see what's in other shop windows that you really like. Take notes, take pictures!

Badge link

Clothing

Be a walking, talking display! Use fabric paint to put your message on T-shirts for you and your friends to wear.

Video

Be a director! Want something extra, maybe for a stand at a fair? Create a short film clip in advance – with music, singing, dancing and games – that you can play on a loop alongside your display. Or it could be the display!

1951 During Brownie Exhibition Week, over 5,000 people come to view displays made by Brownies at guiding's headquarters in London.

Live display

Doing a live demonstration of a skill, game or other? Make sure you rehearse lots before the big day so you feel ready and confident!

Global Brownie

No matter where you live, you are connected to other people all over the world!

Draw yourself below and answer the questions about you and your global links!

Then see if you can find each country on the map and colour it in.

If you do ballet, you probably know some French words!

The words 'pyjamas' and 'jungle' are from Hindi, which is spoken in parts of India.

My *one of* favourite animal is the

...... *dolphin* ......

......

which lives in ..... *Ocean* .....

......

My favourite food is..... *bread* .....

which comes from ......

I live in ......Edinburgh..................

I have relatives in .....Cranky...............

1957 Brownies do six World Good Turns to mark the Baden-Powell Centenary year.

My name is from ...Greece..

....

and it means ....

....

....

(ask your family if you don't know).

Many words which tell musicians how to play come from Italian – 'forte' ('for-tay') means 'loud' and 'dolce' ('dol-chay') means 'sweetly'.

My clothes were made in......Baden...........................
(check the label if you can!) and I like to go on holiday to

.......lots...are.places.like............cregg..........

29

Annuals through the years

Take a peek at Brownie Annuals from the past.

1959 Brownie Annual

This was the very first *Brownie Annual* (published in time for the Christmas of 1958). The pages were black and white, and it had lots and lots of exciting stories, including one about children putting out a bushfire all by themselves! We don't recommend you do this, however – be sensible, stay out of harm's way and tell an adult, who will call emergency services to deal with it.

1974 Brownie Annual

This Annual was published on Brownies' 60th birthday. By then the annual had some pages in colour, lots more puzzles and photos of Brownies doing Brownie things. But Brownie wear still hadn't changed very much!

1984 Brownie Annual

This Annual came out when Brownies turned 70. If your mum or aunt was at Brownies they might remember it! It was mostly in colour – hurrah! It had cool facts about other Brownies around the world, activities with badge links and introduced the Conservation badge (which later became the Environment badge).

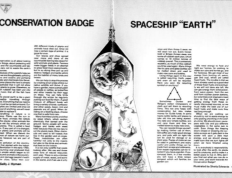

1994 Brownie Annual

The 80th birthday Annual was full of illustrations. It had Brownies showing you how to be sporty and active as well as how to bake pizza (as you do when in Milan!), and cool science experiments. Brownie tops were now yellow, and a lot less itchy!

2004 Brownie Annual

This Annual was from ten years ago, when Brownies turned 90. It looked a lot like today's annuals. It had Brownies in modern Brownie wear, recipe treats for all seasons, a photostory about being a Brownie buddy, and pictures of lots of cute, furry animals!

Superstars

When we think of space exploration, most people think of Neil Armstrong on the moon in 1969. But six years earlier, Valentina Tereshkova made history by being the first woman to travel in space. Here are a few more fearless women to inspire you to be adventurous, brave, clever and strong!

Past

Elizabeth I

At a time when women were expected to get married and do what their husbands told them, Queen Elizabeth I refused to find herself a King and ruled England, Ireland and Wales for 45 years all by herself.

© Alamy

Emmeline Pankhurst

Did you know that until 1918 women in Britain weren't allowed to vote? This courageous woman led a long, hard campaign and won the right for you to vote once you turn 18.

Marie Curie

The Nobel Prize is awarded each year to the very cleverest people in science, literature and peacekeeping. This Polish scientist was the first woman to win the prize, and also the only one ever to have won it twice!

© Getty Image

© Alamy

Amy Johnson

This young British woman's daredevil flights made her famous. She was the first woman to fly solo to Australia, and was a pilot in the Second World War, until she died tragically in a plane crash.

Present

J.K. Rowling

Everyone loves Harry Potter – the books have sold over 400 million copies! But did you know that 12 publishers actually turned it down at first? This author is proof that you should never give up on your dreams.

© Getty Images

Helen Skelton

This adventurous TV presenter has kayaked the Amazon and cycled to the South Pole. She's also a former Brownie and with Girlguiding members created the world's longest bunting line for Comic Relief!

Jessica Ennis

It takes a lot of strength and determination to be an athlete, and even more so to be an Olympic gold medallist in the heptathlon (seven different sporting events in one)!

© Getty Images

Miranda Hart

She's won loads of awards for making us laugh by falling off furniture, tripping over things and generally making fun of herself. Which is pretty brave, when you think about it!

© Getty Images

Future – YOU!

If you put your mind to it, you can be just as amazing as any of these women. Draw your own face here to remind you of that!

Flower fridge magnets

Letters, bills, shopping lists, notes - people often stick these important things on their fridge so they don't forget about them. Make this pretty felt flower fridge magnet and you can help your family stay organised in style!

You will need

* **sheets of felt in at least three different colours**
* **pen or pencil**
* **scissors**
* **fabric glue**
* **button (with flat back)**
* **magnetic tape**
* **laundry peg (plastic or wooden)**

2 Take your first piece of felt and draw a large flower, then carefully cut it out. Now draw a smaller flower on your second piece of felt and cut that out too.

Be safe

Here's how

1 Choose the colours for your felt flower – you'll need two different colours for the petals and another for the leaf.

Flowers are a popular theme for the 1960s! Young people call for peace in a movement known as 'flower power' and Brownies carry out Flower Good Turns to mark Brownies turning 50 in 1964.

3 Your third piece of felt is for your leaf. Draw the leaf and cut it out.

Be safe

4 Carefully glue the smaller felt flower on top of the larger one, so that you can see both sets of petals.

5 Put glue on one side of the stem of your felt leaf and stick it behind the big flower. You should be able to see the top of the leaf poking out from behind the petals.

6 Now take a button and put enough glue on the back to stick it firmly in the centre of the smaller flower.

7 Cut a strip of magnetic tape the same length as your laundry peg and stick it down one side of the peg. Glue your finished felt flower to the other side of the peg.

8 Leave your flower fridge magnet to dry, and then it's ready to put on the fridge!

Take a tip from a Guide

As a Brownie, you're part of a huge guiding family – and Guides are your big sisters! They have all the best tips on growing up and what to expect when you become a teenager. So take this quiz and find out who's your perfect Guide friend!

1. Before your Brownie meeting starts you can be found:

A) with your Six, chatting about how their week has been

B) rushing around playing a game of 'It'

C) asking your Leader when you can start working on your next badge

D) showing your friends the pretty new bag charm you've made.

2. Have a look at your badges. What's the badge you're most proud of?

A) Your Cook badge – the best part was bringing in a huge cake for your unit to enjoy.

B) Your Watersports badge – it was so much fun getting soaking wet!

C) Your Science investigator badge – you loved finding out about the world around you.

D) Your Designer badge – you know loads about fashion and this was your chance to shine!

3. On Brownie Holiday, you're the Brownie who:

A) everyone comes to when they're feeling homesick or need someone to talk to

B) is always first to try that day's activity, whether it's abseiling, zip wiring or canoeing

C) sometimes slips off for a quiet moment with a good book

D) can't wait for the end-of-camp show – you'll be directing AND starring, of course!

4. What's your favourite thing about being a Brownie?

A) Getting to make new friends and have fun together, especially on Brownie Holiday.

B) Trying out exciting new activities – it's easy to be brave when you're with your friends!

C) Earning new badges and learning new things along the way!

D) Getting messy and creative doing all kinds of craft activities.

5. Brownies turn 100 this year! If you were organising a party for your unit, what would you do?

A) You'd want to ask the rest of your unit first – it's more fun planning together!

B) Some kind of adventure! Perhaps a treasure hunt or a trip to a theme park.

C) Eat food from different countries to celebrate Brownies all over the world.

D) It'd definitely be a fancy dress party! Think of the fun you'd all have designing costumes!

Now add up your answers – count how many of each letter you got.

Illustrated by Emma McCann

If you got mostly As:
Your Guide friend is Caring and Sharing Claire!

Claire is really excited to meet you because she loves making new friends – just like you do! She enjoys sleepovers where she can stay up late swapping stories and giving great advice.

Claire's top tip: 'Best friends are the ones who love you just for being you.'

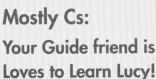
The **1960s** also sees the rise of teenage culture, with teens making their voices heard – usually at concerts screaming at their favourite pop stars!

Mostly Bs:
Your Guide friend is Action and Adventure Amina!

If you can keep up, you'll have an amazing time with Amina, who loves doing anything sporty or adventurous. But you should have no problem with that, since you're as full of energy as she is!

Amina's top tip: 'Don't let anyone tell you that being sporty is just for boys – we're just as good at it as they are!'

Mostly Cs:
Your Guide friend is Loves to Learn Lucy!

Life with Lucy is never boring – she's always got a new fact to amaze you with. Though perhaps you can teach her a thing or two, given how many badges you've got!

Lucy's top tip: 'Trying hard at school doesn't make you a geek; it makes you an interesting person with lots to say.'

Mostly Ds:
Your Guide friend is Super Stylish Suki!

With both of your creative skills combined, you and Suki are going to make a great team. Whether it's acting, singing, dancing or fashion that you love, Suki will know how to add that extra sparkle.

Suki's top tip: 'Buy clothes because you really love them and they suit you, not because they're fashionable and all your friends have them.'

Detective Brownie and the missing jubilee gem

Scruff sniffed at the note, but I was one step ahead of him. I knew that there was some birthday bash at the museum with exhibits that no crook could resist. 'Come on, old buddy – we've got a case to close.'

We hit the streets hard – it was starting to rain and Scruff was in no mood to get his coat wet. We reached the museum in double-quick time, but the main doors were only for the party guests. 'Rats!' Scruff started heading towards the back of the building. It looked like he had a lead, and not just his walking one. There were three smaller doors – but which one leads to the gallery?

It had been a long day and I was just closing up. I was looking forward to an evening with my old pal Scruff, and maybe a tall drink of lemonade, when a note slid under the door. It wasn't like any other note – it was like having a chinwag with a calculator:

Decode the note:
23 5 23 9 12 12 19 20 5 1 12 20 8
5 4 9 1 13 15 14 4

A 1	B 2	C 3	D 4	E 5
F 6	G 7	H 8	I 9	J 10
K 11	L 12	M 13	N 14	O 15
P 16	Q 17	R 18	S 19	T 20
U 21	V 22	W 23	X 24	Y 25
Z 26				

Illustrated by Rémy Simard

Which door should DB use?

It was dark on the stairs, but I had no fear. Broken lightbulbs are no match for Detective Brownie. I led Scruff through a door into one of the galleries.

'Well, if it isn't my old pal, Detective B.'

I jumped and turned around to see Dr Jones, the museum's director, stepping out from between a row of old statues. She looked none too friendly and Scruff's muddy paw-prints on her shiny museum floor didn't help.

'We meet again, Dr J. It wouldn't be you who sent me this message?' I waved the note at her. She shook her head.

'I got a note too, but I can't read mine.'

Decode the note:
διαμονδ ισ γονε

α	a	ν	n
η	c	ο	o
δ	d	π	r
ε	e	ρ	r
ζ	f	σ	s
γ	g	τ	t
θ	h	υ	u
ι	i	φ	v
κ	k	χ	x
λ	l	ψ	y
μ	m	ω	z

I looked over the note and sent Dr Jones back to the birthday party to look after her guests. This was no time to dilly dally – the crooks had already stolen the goods! I needed to gather evidence, but where were they keeping this gem? I was stumped, but I looked down at Scruff's muddy pawprints.

Which floor is the diamond on?

'Attaboy, Scruff!'

I picked up the pace and ran through the different exhibits, passing Egyptian mummies, Viking longboats and a Victorian steam engine. I hit a dead end – just a big locked door between me and solving my case. There was a keypad on the wall – but what was the code?

What is the code?

I had to get in fast before the thieves could make their getaway, ruining Dr Jones' party. The party! The *birthday* party. I knew what the code would be. All I had to do was work out how to turn those letters into numbers. I whipped out my phone, looked at the letters on the keys and typed in the word 'BIRTHDAY'.

The doors swung open and I gasped. The diamond was right there, sitting on a velvet cushion, shining brighter than a Christmas tree on fire. This case was getting more confusing by the minute. My phone buzzed and I looked at the message.

Decode the message: gobackdownstairsthisexhibitisafake

The double-crossers! They had stolen the jewel and replaced it with a fake. Scruff and I went back downstairs and saw Dr Jones leaving the party in a hurry.

'Dr Jones! Dr Jones! They got the goods!' But she didn't stop when I called her. She had a big backpack over her shoulder – the zip was slightly open and I could see something very shiny in the bag. I had found the thief after all! Scruff bounded towards her and blocked her path. We had caught the culprit red-handed! All the party guests stared as Dr Jones handed over the bag with the real diamond in it.

'Three cheers for Detective Brownie! Come and join the party!'

'Thank you, but I already have plans.' I looked down at Scruff. 'Now how about that lemonade?'

How did you do?
Answers on page 76.

40

Detective Brownie's sleuthing tips

✱ Keep a diary of anything suspicious – make a note of what you saw, where and when. Take photos if you can, or draw pictures.

✱ Remember that anything can be evidence – don't ignore even the smallest detail!

✱ Play memory games to improve your observation skills. Ask a friend to move or change something in a room without you knowing, and see if you can spot it when you come back in.

✱ Keep a disguise handy – you could hide behind a book or umbrella, or wear a hat or pair of glasses.

✱ Practise moving as quietly as you can – wear soft shoes and clothes that don't make a noise, and avoid treading on squeaky stairs or crunchy leaves.

✱ If you're in an area you don't know, look behind you every few minutes and take a mental picture so you can find your way home again!

✱ Learn to read faces – watch people closely while they tell the truth, and when you know they're lying. Do they scratch their nose or play with their hair? Look to the left? Blink more often?

✱ Recruit some friends as detectives too – the more eyes and ears on the case the better!

41

Brain benders!

Dizzy dominoes

In dominoes, you add pieces by matching up ends with the same number of dots. But some of the pieces have fallen on the floor! Which ones complete the game?

Mixed-up meals

Guess the food from each of the words and pictures below.

a) HOtoadLE

b) bread

c) ggegsgsgegse

d)
```
M E
A
L
```

e) tr🍩🍩t

f) bean bean bean

42

Mind how you go!

How many of these ways to get around can you find in the wordsearch?

* hop
* drive
* fly
* skip
* wander
* dawdle
* jump
* walk
* skate
* scoot
* cycle
* swim

S	E	S	C	O	O	T	D	I	P
N	W	U	E	Y	C	A	R	S	K
F	R	A	W	E	Y	P	I	K	S
O	I	T	N	L	C	F	V	A	H
S	B	E	C	D	L	U	E	T	G
W	N	C	D	W	E	D	R	E	J
I	A	C	L	A	O	R	N	M	U
M	F	L	Y	D	T	A	D	K	M
L	Y	E	K	P	L	R	H	O	P
D	C	B	O	M	G	W	M	R	I

Check pages 76–77 to see how you did!

Mystery Sixes

Unscramble these anagrams to find the Brownie Sixes.

FEL ey

LIQUERRS squirrels

SIRPET sprite

PAURELENCH leprauchan

TRIBBA rabbit

HOGGEDEH Hedghog

Piggy in the middle

Can you find the word that can be added to each pair to make two new words? So adding 'finger' to the first pair makes 'fish finger' and 'finger puppet'!

* fish ginger puppet

a) sea horse shoe

b) sand ... clip

c) wisdom ... fairy

d) rain ... tie

e) chocolate ... badge

f) library ... mark

g) dining ... tennis

h) night ... switch

i) sweet ... flakes

The next big thing!

It's the newest invention - and everyone will want one! But what is it?

Read the advert below and each time you come to a gap, roll a dice or pick a number to find out which word to use. Then draw a picture of what this crazy invention might look like – and don't forget to give it a name!

Introducing our latest invention. It's weird, it's wonderful and it will change your life. It's the ___invisible___ (pick a word from list A)_____ way to ___do___ (B)___get to school on time___ do your homework. But it gets better - it works ___whatever___ (C)___the weather___! So don't delay, buy one today!

The **1980s** see great advances in technology. Personal computers become widely available and the first mobile phone appears - its batteries last just 30 minutes and take ten hours to charge!

Draw a picture of your invention. Does it have a screen? Buttons? Legs? Does it need batteries, wind or clockwork to make it work? Or something else? How big is it? What colour?

My invention is called:

invisable

A	B	C
1. new	1. walk your dog	1. using microwaves
2. invisible	2. play music	2. underwater
3. fast	3. get to school in 20 seconds	3. while you sleep
4. tasty	4. do your homework	4. with robotic arms
5. easy	5. record your dreams	5. in space
6. solar-powered	6. look after your little sister	6. whatever the weather

Terrific tea

Use tea to make an ancient-looking treasure map – or some amazing scented pictures!

You will need

* paper
* different types of teabags – try herbal ones like mint, blackberry or rosehip
* cup of warm water
* paper towels
* instant coffee (optional)
* pen
* scissors

What to do

1 Crumple up the paper and flatten it out again.

3 Once the paper is covered in tea, put it somewhere warm on some paper towels to dry.

2 Carefully dip a teabag in the warm water and wipe it over the surface of the paper. The paper will start to go brown, and the tea will collect in the wrinkles so it looks really old!

Illustrated by Nancy Meyers

4 When it's almost dry, sprinkle a few grains of instant coffee over the surface for added effect, if you want.

Top tips!

Try this with other teabags to make paper in lots of different colours. When the paper is dry, can you still smell the different types of tea? Why not cut shapes out of each colour and make a cool picture that smells great too?

5 Once it's dry, draw on your treasure map!

1984 The National Brownie Tea-making Fortnight begins on 14 April – each Brownie is challenged to make 30 cups of tea for the public!

We're endangered too!

Some animals are 'endangered' – there aren't many of them left, because they are hunted or the places where they live are being destroyed. You probably already know about tigers, pandas and elephants – but have you heard of any of these amazing animals?

Long-beaked echidna

I live in Papua New Guinea and even though I'm a mammal, like dogs or humans, I have a beak instead of teeth and lay eggs like a bird! I may look cute and fluffy, but watch out – I have spines like a hedgehog, and if you scare me I can roll into a ball.

Matschie's tree kangaroo

I'm a Roo, and I live in a tree! You can find me in rainforests in Australia, West Papua and Papua New Guinea. As a marsupial, I've got a pouch for carrying my joeys. I prefer climbing around as I'm pretty clumsy on the ground! I'm also super tough – I can jump down from 18 metres up without getting so much as a scratch!

In the 1980s people become more concerned about the health of our planet, and taking action about it.

Badge link

friend to animals

Chinese giant salamander

I'm related to frogs and toads but I can grow to nearly two metres long – taller than a grown-up human! My eyesight isn't very good, but I can feel vibrations in the water using special spots on my skin. Did you know that I breathe through my skin, and I can bark, hiss or cry like a baby?

Ozark big-eared bat

Aren't my ears splendid? They take up a quarter of my height! I live in the United States and, like a lot of my bat cousins, I like to make my home inside caves. My favourite food is moths, lots of moths! I have to eat plenty of them to survive when I hibernate and sleep through the winter.

Northern bald ibis

I may have a wrinkly bald head but the Ancient Egyptians thought my shiny black feathers were very beautiful! I live in Morocco and Turkey, and I use my long beak to dig around in the soil for beetles, insects and lizards.

My web world

Do you love websites with a world of their own? With cute characters to adopt, games for your pets to play, crazy food to 'buy' and homes to furnish? Why not create your own web world?

1 Start with a set of adorable characters – choose naughty and nice ones to make it fun. They could be little people, monsters, fluffy animals or a group of Brownie friends. What will you call them? Will they have magical powers?

2 Think about where your new friends live. What sort of world is it – colourful and full of adventure or with mysteries and challenges at every turn?

3 What happens when your friends meet? Is it trouble with a capital 'T' or are they on a mission to save the world?

4 What sort of rewards can your friends win and what can they do with them – buy food, a new outfit, a better super power?

5 Invent quizzes for your friends to try or think about adventures they can go on together.

6 Come up with ways to keep your friends happy – we all need love!

1990 Sir Tim Berners-Lee invents the World Wide Web, otherwise known as the internet, and gives it to the world for free!

My Brownie Web Safe Code
When using the World Wide Web I promise:

* To agree rules with my parents or carers about the best way for me to use my devices (computer, phone, games console) and the internet.

* To keep my personal information safe and share it only if I have permission to do so (my full name, my home or school address, my phone number, my email address).

* Not to agree to meet anyone who I contact on the internet, unless my parents or carers say it is all right and go with me.

* To share my photos and videos only with people I trust online, and always ask permission before I upload them.

* To tell my parents, carers, teacher or Leader if something online worries or upsets me.

* To download files on to my devices only with permission from a parent or carer.

* To think carefully about what I read, hear and see online, and not to trust information unless I have checked it on other websites, or in books, or have asked an adult about it.

Web safe

Top Tips!

* **Create your world on the biggest piece of paper you can find. Draw your characters on another sheet then cut them out so they can move around.**

* **To create really cute friends make sure you give them big, shiny eyes.**

* **Let your imagination run wild! Your friends could live anywhere – up in the trees, in jellybean houses, on an ice cap, in space!**

* **If you're handy with modelling clay, why not create 3D characters to play with?**

* **Visit the Brownie website (www.girlguiding.org. uk/brownies) – it's full of games to play and will give you more ideas!**

Book quiz

1997 The first Harry Potter book, Harry Potter and the Philosopher's Stone, comes out!

Are you a book worm? Try out this quiz about stories new and old.

1 In Dr Seuss's *The Cat in the Hat,* how many Things are there? *2*

2 Name Horrid Henry's brother. *perfect peter*

3 What is the name of Peter Rabbit's cousin? *benjamin*

4 In Roald Dahl's *Danny the Champion of the World,* what job does Danny's dad do?

5 Name Joe Spud's new best friend in *Billionaire Boy.*

6 What colour are the wings on Enid Blyton's *Wishing Chair*?

7 Why does Pippi Longstocking have such big shoes?

8 Who does Harry Potter share his birthday with?

9 Where does Dave find Dogger?

10 In *The Butterfly Lion,* why does Bertie run away from school?

11 Who wrote about Hetty Feather? *Jacqueline Wilson*

12 In the *Just So Stories,* how does the Elephant Child get his trunk?

13 Which country is Mrs Pepperpot from? *Norway*

14 Milly-Molly-Mandy wears pink-and-white-striped cotton in the summer. What does she wear in the winter? *red serge*

15 How do Peter, Susan, Edmund and Lucy get to Narnia? *magic wardrobe*

16 In *Alice in Wonderland,* what is Alice doing before she sees the White Rabbit? *Sitting with her sister on the river bank*

17 What *did* Katy do next? *Travelled to Europe*

18 Who is the Wimpy Kid? *Greg Heffley*

19 In *The Family from One End Street,* how many brothers and sisters does Lily Rose have? *six kate jim john the twins jo peg william*

20 What is the name of the porter in *The Railway Children*? *perks*

Feeling inspired? Why not get down to your local library with a list of books you'd like to read and bury yourself in a book?

Check page 77 to see how you did!

The books

Enid Blyton,
The Wishing Chair

Joyce Lankester Brisley, ✓
Milly-Molly-Mandy series

Lewis Carroll, ✓
*Alice's Adventures
in Wonderland*

Susan Coolidge, *What
Katy Did* series ✓

Roald Dahl, *Danny the
Champion of the World*

Eve Garnett, ✓
*The Family from One End
Street*

Shirley Hughes, *Dogger*

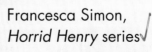

Jeff Kinney, *Diary of
a Wimpy Kid* ✓

Rudyard Kipling,
Just So Stories

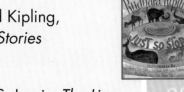

C.S. Lewis, *The Lion,
the Witch and the
Wardrobe* ✓

Astrid Lindgren,
Pippi Longstocking

Michael Morpurgo,
The Butterfly Lion ✓

E. Nesbit,
The Railway Children

Beatrix Potter, *The Tale
of Benjamin Bunny* ✓

Alf Prøysen,
Mrs Pepperpot series ✓

J.K. Rowling,
Harry Potter series ✓

Dr Seuss,
The Cat in the Hat ✓

Francesca Simon,
Horrid Henry series ✓

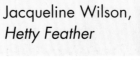

David Walliams,
Billionaire Boy

Jacqueline Wilson,
Hetty Feather

Let's get dipping!

Whether you like to dip carrot sticks or cheese straws, you'll love these tasty dips.

You will need

* * half a cucumber
* * 150ml natural yoghurt
* * 10ml (2 tsp) olive oil
* * 15ml (1 tbsp) fresh mint
* * half a garlic clove

* * scales and measuring spoons
* * vegetable knife
* * chopping board
* * serving bowl
* * dinner knife
* * spoon

Tzatziki

Greek people eat this dip before a meal with bread but you can have it as a healthy snack, perhaps with strips of pitta bread.

What to do

1 Carefully chop the cucumber, on the chopping board into pieces and put in the serving bowl.

Be safe

2 Pour the yoghurt and olive oil over the cucumber.

3 Carefully chop the mint into tiny pieces and add it to the bowl.

Be safe

4 Using the side of the blade of the dinner knife, crush your half garlic clove and add the squashed garlic to the bowl.

Be safe

5 Stir the mixture with a spoon and serve.

Green Mexican dip

This dip uses avocado, which goes brown quite quickly, so don't make it until you need it.

What to do

1 Carefully cut the avocado in half and take out the stone.

Be safe

2 Scoop the avocado flesh out of its skin into the serving bowl and mash with the fork.

3 Add the lime juice to the avocado and mix.

4 Carefully chop the pepper into small pieces and add to the avocado.

Be safe

5 Mix the dip with a spoon before serving.

Instant dips

* Hummus
* Cream cheese
* Chocolate spread
* Custard
* Peanut butter

Don't forget kitchen safety! Wash your hands, tie back long hair and put an apron on before you start. Ask an adult to supervise you when you use a knife. Lastly, check if anyone has food allergies to any of your ingredients.

Be safe

Bits to dip

Why not try:

* apple slices
* raw pea pods
* cucumber sticks
* baby sweetcorn
* breadsticks
* celery
* pepper slices
* strawberries
* fingers!

More dippy ideas

Why not stir up:

* cream cheese and pesto
* plain yoghurt and chopped fruit
* avocado and hummus
* mayonnaise and mild curry paste
* crème fraîche and chopped chives.

Organically grown food becomes more and more popular in the 1990s.

Cool calendars

1

Calendars are used to organise days. Periods in a calendar are organised into months and years, usually following how the sun or moon moves. The Gregorian calendar is the international standard which is most widely used, but many other calendars – such as Mayan, Islamic, Hindu and Buddhist – also exist.

Fun calendar facts

Many people gathered to celebrate the end of a 5,126-year-long cycle of the Mayan calendar which ended on 21 December 2012. Some believed that when the cycle came to an end so too would the world! Thankfully the predictions proved to be wrong!

Most calendars have 12 or 13 months in each year as they are lunar or solar calendars. This means that they follow the motion of the moon or the sun.

Researchers have discovered sticks of bone, wood and stone with notches marked on them from the Paleolithic era (Stone Age). This means that people counted the days in relation to the moon's phases as early as about 600,000 or 700,000 years ago!

The Islamic calendar has 12 months but only 354 days – do you know how many days there are in the Gregorian calendar?

Months of the year wordsearch

Hidden to the right are all the months of the year. How many can you find? And how quickly? Check page 77 to see how you did.

E	N	O	V	E	M	B	E	R	R	Y	M
D	N	A	P	B	I	T	H	Z	W	Q	S
L	L	U	F	H	A	C	U	O	F	S	E
M	E	G	J	X	R	A	O	I	E	N	P
D	V	U	E	A	K	J	Q	W	B	B	T
E	O	S	M	D	N	T	P	N	R	M	E
C	Q	T	A	O	I	U	K	O	U	S	M
E	A	D	Y	L	U	J	A	E	A	C	B
M	S	H	K	S	P	V	P	R	R	S	E
B	O	C	T	O	B	E	R	N	Y	A	R
E	C	H	A	K	J	B	I	C	H	N	X
R	W	Z	H	F	W	B	L	P	A	D	T

The year 2000 is special as it is the start of a new calendar millennium – which happens only once every 1,000 years!

Badge link

What's in a name?

The month of June was named in honour of the Roman queen of the gods – Juno.

The month of April comes from the Latin word 'aperire' meaning 'to open' – this is the month when the flower buds begin to open.

Can you find out how the other months of the year came to be named?

新年快乐! (sheen knee-en kwai l-uh!)

Happy New Year! Chinese New Year is the most important and oldest celebration in the Chinese calendar, and festivities last for two weeks!

A rhyme to remember

Need a little help to remember how many days there are in each month? Check out this rhyme for a reminder! It's thought to date back to at least the 16th century – do you think it's still useful today?

Thirty days hath September,
April, June and November.
All the rest have thirty-one,
Excepting February alone
Which has twenty-eight days clear
And twenty-nine in each leap year.

MONKEY

Did you know?

The date of the Chinese New Year changes each year; this year it falls on 31 January 2014.

The Chinese Zodiac has 12 animal signs (each year is a different animal) and depending on the year you were born, you are believed to have the various character traits of that year's animal.

This year, 2014, is the year of the horse. If you were born in the year of the horse you are meant to be cheerful, energetic and talented, but tend to talk too much and can be impatient! Can you find out which animal year it was when you were born? How much are you like your animal?

HORSE

OX

DOG

57

Brownies in action!

For 100 years Brownies have always risen to a challenge! Here are some examples of Brownies taking action, past and present.

2002 Nations around the world agree to support the Millennium Development Goals and help millions out of poverty by 2015. Between **2008** and **2009** **296,591** Girlguiding members help through Changing the World.

Hello, my name is Peggy!

My name is Katie!

The helpful Brownie (1914–1918)

'I helped to raise money to build the Girlguiding headquarters in London! It wasn't just me and my Brownie friends of course – everyone in guiding got involved and did their bit. We launched an SOS appeal, "Short of Stuff", and girls all around the world gave something to the fund for the new building.'

The war effort Brownie (1940)

Hello! I'm Carrie!

The resourceful Brownie (1930s)

'When war broke out, my Brownie friends and I were keen to help in any way we could. We did lots of things to lend a hand. I joined the National Egg Collection scheme, collecting freshly laid eggs to send to our British soldiers wounded in France, as well as doing cooking, needlework and laundry for places like hospitals – the skills I learned to earn my badges really helped out there!'

'During Guide Gift Week we raised a whopping £50,000 to put towards the war effort. Our fundraising included donating our pocket money and doing odd jobs like weeding, painting or minding babies. We used it to buy two air ambulances, 20 naval ambulances, a motor lifeboat and more!'

Illustrated by Emma McCann

58

The environmentally
friendly Brownie (1981)

Hi, I'm Ayesha!

'The Adopt and Cherish campaign was launched to encourage us all to improve and maintain neglected local areas and to do our bit for the environment. My unit and I adopted a scruffy piece of land next to our local community centre and transformed it into an area where people wanted to spend time! We cleared the rubbish, cut back the overgrown hedges and planted lots of cheerful flowers and plants. The local garden centre even donated a bench!'

Hey there!
I'm Mia!

Hello! I'm Beth!

'Last year I took part in the Safe Haven project for the Red Cross as part of Girls in Action. We wrote welcome letters and postcards to young refugees arriving in the UK to make them feel less scared about being in a strange country. There were lots of projects to choose from and different charities to support, like Plan UK and Railway Children. We really felt like we had made a difference to the lives of these girls and young women coming to the UK.'

The welcoming
Brownie (2013)

The fundraising
Brownie (1995)

'I took part in the Week of Water Wacky Wash! My Brownie friends and I washed Flossy the elephant at Dudley Zoo - we were all soaked, but raised lots of money and had loads of messy water fun! The money we raised provided life-saving water supplies for thousands of people in Africa and Asia. On average, £15,000 was raised each year over the six-year campaign.'

Slumber well!

Children between 5 and 12 need 10 to 11 hours of sleep each night. How much sleep do you get? We all need sleep to keep us happy, healthy and doing our best!

How well do you sleep?

Answer each of the following statements with 'true' or 'false'.

1 I wake up feeling refreshed and ready for the day. **True or false?**
2 I hardly ever feel tired during the day. **True or false?**
3 I go to bed at around the same time every night. **True or false?**
4 My bedroom is quiet, dark and comfortable at bedtime. **True or false?**
5 I think that getting a good night's sleep is as important as a good diet and exercise. **True or false?**
6 I follow the same routine before going to bed every night. **True or false?**
7 I find it easy to concentrate and pay attention at school. **True or false?**
8 I do something relaxing before bedtime like reading or listening to soothing music. **True or false?**
9 I try not to eat a big meal close to my bedtime, but I might have a small snack. **True or false?**
10 I don't watch TV or play computer games in bed. **True or false?**

How did you do?

Mostly true: Sleeping beauty!
Well done! You're getting plenty of sleep! That means that your body can grow and repair itself, you'll do well at school and you'll feel happy and full of energy!

Equally true and false: So-so sleeper!
The sleep you're getting is okay, but you could do with a bit more! Try going to bed 30 minutes earlier each night and break some of those bad bedtime habits!

Mostly false: Sleepyhead!
Oh no! You're not getting enough sleep! That makes us feel tired, but that's not all – have you ever felt grumpy or tearful after having too little sleep? We need sleep to keep us feeling happy as well as healthy!

Did you know?

Some animals spend up to 22 hours a day sleeping! Can you guess which animal is the sleepiest?*

Badge link

2007 Brownies hold a world-record sleepover at the BT Tower in London!

Top tips for sweet slumbers

✻ Have a bedtime routine.

✻ Try to go to bed at the same time each night.

✻ Avoid big meals before bed – have a snack instead.

✻ Switch off the TV and computer games at least one hour before bedtime.

✻ Exercise and eat healthily during the day.

✻ Do something relaxing before going to sleep.

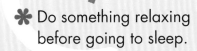

*The koala can sleep up to 22 hours a day!

Win an amazing day out with **LEGO** *Friends*

Would you like to win a once-in-a-lifetime day out for you and your unit at LEGOLAND Windsor?

Well, thanks to LEGO Friends, you could!

For a chance to win this incredible prize you have to send us a photo of you and your unit with a LEGO creation of your very own. Also, in no more than 30 words, tell us about a new challenge you are looking forward to or have completed, or a new skill you have gained. Perhaps your unit helped you learn your new skill? Or you overcame a challenge with your unit's help? Whatever your story, we want to hear about your proudest achievement!

And if you fancy taking on more challenges, have a go at the Challenge Chart your LEGO Friends have come up with opposite!

The prize

The best entry will win tickets for the whole unit (including Leaders) to spend the day at LEGOLAND Windsor Resort. The prize will include entry to the park for your unit, with over 55 rides and attractions. You will get priority entrance to your favourite ride, a visit from a very special character, the opportunity to earn your very first 'driving licence', souvenir goodie bags and travel expenses.

How to enter

Post your competition entry in by 28 February 2014 with your name, your Leader's name, your unit's name and your District or Division's name to:

Brownie Annual 2014 Competition
Girlguiding
17–19 Buckingham Palace Road
London SW1W 0PT

LEGO® Friends

Challenge Chart!

The LEGO® Friends have come up with loads of ideas to have some fun. Have a go at one activity a day and record what you did and who you did it with.

		✗ / ✔	❀ / ★ / 🦋
Monday	Host your own talent show.	✔	★
Tuesday	Learn a magic trick.	✔	★
Wednesday	Play football in your garden or in the park.	✔	❀
Thursday	Try out a new hair style.	✔	★
Friday	Take care of your pet or help with someone else's.	✔	★
Saturday	Sing a song for your family.		
Sunday	Practise your swimming.		

❀ = I did it on my own.

★ = I did it with my family.

🦋 = I did it with a friend.

Olivia

Stephanie

Mia

Andrea **Emma**

New!

Web safe

The LEGO® Friends live in the beautiful Heartlake City. Find out about all their adventures at www.LEGOfriends.com

Olivia's Newborn Foal • Stephanie's Soccer Practice • Emma's Karate Class • Mia's Magic Tricks • Rehearsal Stage

© LEGO and the LEGO logo are trademarks of the LEGO Group. ©2013 The LEGO Group.

The Big Brownie Birthday cake

You will need

* 220g self-raising flour
* 220g caster sugar
* 220g butter or margarine
* 3 eggs
* 30g cocoa powder
* chocolate chips
* 100ml milk
* a tin of mango pulp
* 200g icing sugar

* weighing scale
* 2 mixing bowls
* wooden spoon
* 2 cake tins

What better way to celebrate 100 years of Brownies than by making this special Big Brownie Birthday cake for your unit!

1 Mix the flour and sugar in a bowl using a wooden spoon.

2 Add the butter and eggs and beat together, making sure no lumps form.

3 Divide the mixture evenly between two bowls.

4 Mix the cocoa powder and chocolate chips into one bowl of mixture and stir in the milk gradually.

5 Mix 100ml of mango pulp into the other mixture.

6 Pour each cake mix into a cake tin.

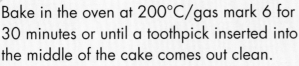

7 Bake in the oven at 200°C/gas mark 6 for 30 minutes or until a toothpick inserted into the middle of the cake comes out clean.

Badge link

8 Cool the cake tins on a wire rack.

9 To make the icing, mix two tablespoons of mango pulp with the icing sugar. It should be bright yellow and stiff enough to spread.

10 Remove the cooled cakes from the tins. Place chocolate cake as the bottom layer and spread half of the icing evenly on top. Place the yellow cake as the top layer and spread the remaining mango icing evenly on top. Enjoy!

Top Tips!

Decorate your Big Brownie Birthday cake with edible sparkles or glitter to make it really special! If you can't find tinned mango pulp, buy a fresh mango instead and mash it! Or put yellow food colouring in the cake mixture, and mix food colouring and water with icing sugar to achieve the Brownie yellow.

The Big Brownie Birthday research

…and because Brownies are 100 years old, we're going to have a party – and everyone can join in! What do you think we should do to celebrate?

My dad is really good at baking. He could make us a birthday cake!

But what can I do?

And I can paint some posters to decorate the walls!

Badge link

④

Why don't you see what you can find out about the history of Brownies? I'm sure your friends will help!

That's all right. It's really interesting to find out what Brownies used to be like!

Listen to this!

⑤

Thanks for helping me with my research.

We should show the other Brownies photos of these old uniforms!

Later that week...

At the next Brownie meeting...

⑥

Are you ready to show us what you found out?

I think so!

Did you know that Brownies used to be called Rosebuds? They didn't like the name and asked for it to be changed!

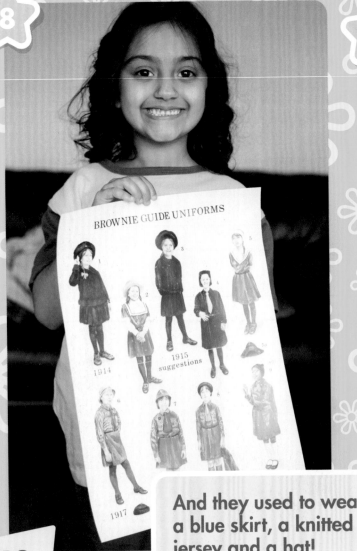

And they used to wear a blue skirt, a knitted jersey and a hat!

The first Brownie Annual was published in 1958 – that's 56 years ago!

10

Thanks for telling us all about the history of Brownies.

I never knew that!

I couldn't have done it without help from my friends!

11

And now it's time to celebrate! Does anyone want some cake?

12

Yes please!

BSI: Brownie Science Investigation

It's time to put on your activity apron and get your fingers stuck in with some experiments!

Liquid or solid?

You will need

* 450g cornflour
* water

* large mixing bowl
* baking tray
* newspaper or plastic to cover the floor

What to do

1 Put the cornflour and roughly one to two cups of water in a bowl. Mix together with your hands until it has the consistency of honey.

2 Pour the mixture on to the baking tray.

3 Try to roll the mixture between your palms to make a ball. If you're feeling brave, hold a hand flat over the gloop, then slap it as hard as you can. What happens? Did the mixture act like a solid sometimes and a liquid at other times?

IMPORTANT Do not pour this mixture down the plughole – it will clog the pipes and block the drain. Pour the mixture into a plastic bag and dispose of it in the bin.

These activities are
supported by

Rolls-Royce

to inspire our future scientists
and engineers.

Badge link

The science bit

What you made is an example of a suspension – a mixture of two substances, a solid dispersed in a liquid. The grains of starch in the cornflour do not dissolve in the water but are instead suspended and spread out.

When you add pressure, like squeezing the mixture in your hand, it causes the cornstarch molecules to lock together, becoming like a solid. The starch molecules hold their shape when this pressure is applied, but because water is trapped between the molecules, when the pressure is released, it returns to a liquid state.

In science terms, it is a non-Newtonian fluid, meaning that when Sir Isaac Newton said liquids flow at consistent, predictable rates he wasn't talking about cornstarch gloop! Non-Newtonian fluid can act almost like a solid and flow like a liquid.

Stunning sundials

You will need

* **shoebox**
* **pen**
* **CD**
* **screwdriver**
* **long, straight stick**
  (for example,
  a bamboo cane)
* **sticky tape**
* **compass**
* **clock or watch**

What to do

1 Turn the shoebox so it is standing on one of the short ends.

2 Draw around the CD to mark a circle on the top surface, and mark the middle too.

3 Ask an adult to make a hole in the centre of the circle with the screwdriver.

4

Poke the stick through the hole at an angle and tape the end to the bottom of the box.

5

Find a sunny spot outside and use a compass to make sure the stick is pointing north.

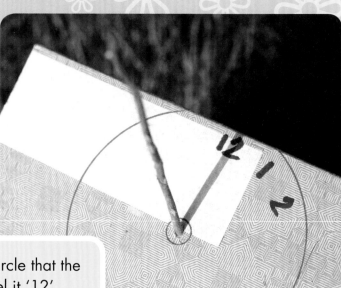

6

At noon, mark the spot on the circle that the stick's shadow crosses, and label it '12'.

7

Repeat each hour for as long as possible, marking each hour on the circle.

8

From now on, as long as the stick is pointing north, you can use the shadow to tell the time. If it falls halfway between the marks for 2pm and 3pm, you can tell it is around 2.30pm!

The science bit

As the Earth travels around the Sun, it appears to rise in the east and set in the west. But in the northern half of the world, it will always be directly south at noon, so will cast a shadow directly north.

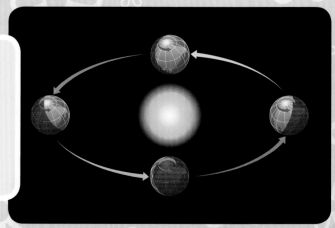

72

Brownie shopping

T-shirt
100% cotton
2111 7-8 years
2112 9-10 years
£7.50

Hoodie
100% cotton
2118 7-8 years
2119 9-10 years
£15

Bracelet
2073 *£4.50*

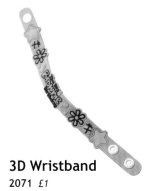

3D Wristband
2071 *£1*

Denim Purse
10x8cm
2058 *£2*

Keyring
Height 6.5cm
2070 *£2*

Resin Bear
Height 5.5cm
2062 *£2*

Teddy Clip
Height 8cm
2064 *£3.50*

Sling Bag
42x29.5cm
2065 *£3.20*

Cards (6)
Glitter decoration,
with envelopes
2085 *£4*

Soft Teddy
Height 15cm (sitting)
2063 *£5.50*

Secret woods

Woodland characters and their other selves...

Highway Badger

At every zebra crossing,
I defend the Highway Code,
The other stripy animal
who helps you cross the road.
You make sure to look both ways
and I'll make the cars stop
With the power of an angry stare
– and a yellow lollipop!

Inspector Fox

I don't think it's a bad thing
when people say I'm sly,
I put my cunning to good use,
now I'm a Private Eye.
Don't believe them when they say
that I'm just out looking for food –
If you see me in the bins,
I'm on the hunt for clues!

Stitch Hedgehog

When it comes to getting crafty,
I don't do things by halves.
I knit jumpers for my friends
and matching hats and gloves
and scarves.
And even though I knit so much
for so many people,
I might run out of wool,
but will not run out of needles!

Engineer Mole

Have you ever wondered
who builds tunnels for the trains?
Or digs out all the waterworks
for wells and pipes and drains?
Who doesn't like the daylight
and sees best when in a hole?
It's me – always underground!
I'm nature's engineer, the mole.

Captain Rabbit

I can sail the seven seas,
battle pirates, fly a plane.
I return my buried treasure
and I go back out again.
When I get back from my journeys,
there's a crowd who whoops and cheers
The only great adventurer
with a tail and two big ears!

Grand Slam Squirrel

Every other morning,
you will find me on the court,
Practising my tennis,
I'm just nutty about the sport.
I'm usually left-handed,
but I know that I can't fail
When I hit the ball over the net
with my bushy tail!

Answers

Pages 12–13 Badge quiz

1 a) Brownie traditions
2 c) Science investigator
3 c) Sports – Big Brownie Birthday special edition!
4 b) Hobbies
5 Five – Finding your way, Fire safety, First aid, First aid advanced, Friend to animals
6 All three – you can use drama or mime to work towards any of these badges
7 Stargazer

Page 15 DB Case Files: The Lost Mascots

1 e) Keyano the Grizzly Bear
2 g) Matilda the Kangaroo
3 d) Mac the 'Scottie'
4 h) Goldie the Kiwi Bird
5 i) Klee Wyck the Orca Whale
6 b) Wira the Orang Utan
7 c) Kit the Cat
8 f) Karak the Cockatoo
9 a) Shera the Tiger

Pages 38–40 Detective Brownie and the missing jubilee gem

Puzzle 1
WE WILL STEAL THE DIAMOND

Puzzle 2
Door 2 – OILTET = TOILET, ALLERGY = GALLERY, FORO = ROOF

Puzzle 3
DIAMOND IS GONE

Puzzle 4
3rd floor

Puzzle 5
24784329

Puzzle 6
GO BACK DOWNSTAIRS THIS EXHIBIT IS A FAKE

Pages 42–43 Brain benders!

Dizzy dominoes
Pieces E, D, C and B

Mixed-up meals
a) Toad in the hole
b) Flatbread
c) Scrambled eggs
d) Square meal
e) Mashed potato
f) Green beans

Mind how you go!

S	E	S	C	O	O	T	D	I	P
N	W	U	E	Y	C	A	R	S	K
F	R	A	W	E	Y	P	I	K	S
O	I	T	N	L	C	F	V	A	H
S	B	E	C	D	L	U	E	T	G
W	N	C	D	W	E	D	R	E	J
I	A	C	L	A	O	R	N	M	U
M	F	L	Y	D	T	A	D	K	M
L	Y	E	K	P	L	R	H	O	P
D	C	B	O	M	G	W	M	R	I

Pages 42–43 Brain benders!

Piggy in the middle
a) horse
b) paper
c) tooth
d) bow
e) brownie
f) book
g) table
h) light
i) corn

Mystery Sixes
FEL (elf)
SIRPET (sprite)
TRIBBA (rabbit)
LIQUERRS (squirrel)
PAURELENCH (leprechaun)
HOGGEDEH (hedgehog)

Pages 52–53 Book quiz

1 Two
2 Perfect Peter
3 Benjamin Bunny
4 Garage mechanic
5 Bob
6 Red
7 So she can wiggle her toes, of course
8 Harry's creator, J.K. Rowling
9 On a toy stall at the school summer fair
10 Bertie wanted to get away from a bully, Basher Beaumont
11 Jacqueline Wilson
12 A crocodile stretched it
13 Norway
14 Red serge
15 Through the wardrobe
16 Sitting with her sister on the river bank
17 Travelled to Europe
18 Greg Heffley
19 Six – Kate, Jim and John (the twins), Jo, Peg and William
20 Perks

Page 56 Months of the year wordsearch

E	N	O	V	E	M	B	E	R	R	Y	M
D	N	A	P	B	I	T	H	Z	W	Q	S
L	L	U	F	H	A	C	U	O	F	S	E
M	E	G	J	X	R	A	O	I	E	N	P
D	V	U	E	A	K	J	Q	W	B	B	T
E	O	S	M	D	N	T	P	N	R	M	E
C	Q	T	A	O	I	U	K	O	U	S	M
E	A	D	Y	L	U	J	A	E	A	C	B
M	S	H	K	S	P	V	P	R	R	S	E
B	O	C	T	O	B	E	R	N	Y	A	R
E	C	H	A	K	J	B	I	C	H	N	X
R	W	Z	H	F	W	B	L	P	A	D	T